Published by

Levonne Gigger and
Gigger² Learning, Instructional Design, & E-learning (GLIDE)
Conyers, Georgia, USA
ISBN: 979-8-992-3450-0-1

Cover Design and book layout: Chidi Ekechukwu
Printed in the United States.

This book is a work of nonfiction. While every effort has been made to ensure accuracy, the author and publisher assume no responsibility for errors or omissions or for damages resulting from the use of information contained herein.

For inquiries, contact:
Levonne Gigger, Gigger² Learning, Instructional Design, & E-learning (GLIDE)
Email: admin@g2lide.com

Acknowledgment

To my baby^2—Layla Heaven-Sage Gigger. This book is written with you in my heart, my kindergarten girl. You were my aspiring YouTube star, always brimming with creativity, boldness, and joy. Though you were taken from me far too soon, your light continues to shine and guide me in everything I do, including this book.

In your honor, a portion of the proceeds from A Globetrotter's Guide to Ghana: An Alphabet Adventure will go to G^{2}L.I.D.E., providing swim scholarships for girls ages 5 to 7—because every little girl deserves to feel safe, empowered, and full of possibility in the water.
This is for you, Layla, and for the dreams you inspire in others.
This is for you, Layla, and all the little girls who will dive into a world of possibilities because of you.

This is for you, Layla, and the waves of change your legacy will create.

Mom^2 loves you forever. ♥

Dedication

With immense gratitude and respect, I dedicate this book to you, Professor Fredoline Anunobi. As the Program Director of the American Institute for Resource and Human Development (AIRHD), your vision and commitment to education have transformed the lives of countless educators, including my own. Your authorship of the grant to the U.S. Department of Education's Fulbright-Hays Program was not just a milestone in securing opportunities for American educators; it was a beacon of hope for cultural exchange and learning.

Your recognition as the recipient of the MOST funded grant by the Fulbright-Hays Program is a testament to your unwavering dedication and passion for empowering others. You have not only paved the way for transformative educational experiences but have also opened your heart and home to me, embracing me as your "daughter."

Thank you for your kindness, guidance, and the familial bond we share. Your support has enriched my life's journey and inspired me to extend that same warmth and dedication to others. This guide is a reflection of the invaluable lessons and experiences I have gained under your mentorship.

As you always say, "Clap for me!" So, let's all take a moment to do just that!

NEW REGIONS OF GHANA AFTER REFERENDUM

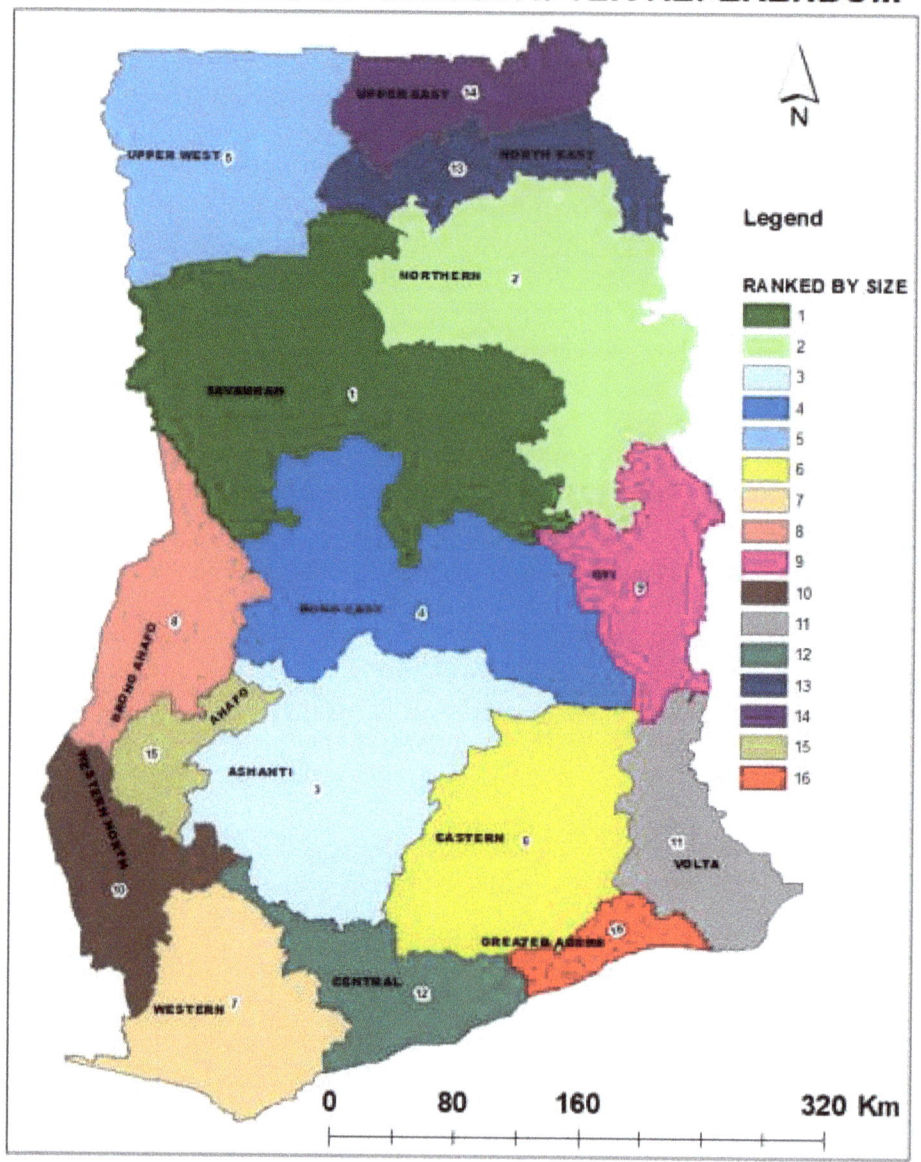

Legend

RANKED BY SIZE

■	1
■	2
■	3
■	4
■	5
■	6
■	7
■	8
■	9
■	10
■	11
■	12
■	13
■	14
■	15
■	16

N

0   80   160   320 Km

BY: SAKO.COM

Akwaaba!

...it's how you say welcome in Twi!

If you're traveling to Ghana, it's
likely you've just landed in the
capital city of Accra.
There is so much to do and see.
Let's see how to travel in Ghana from
A to Z.
In this alphabet book for world
travelers, you'll be introduced to a
place (beae3) or event (dwumadie)
related to the letter and one food
(aduane) or delicacy for the letter.

A is for Aburi.

Adventure awaits in the amazing Aburi Mountains! If you're an adrenaline junkie, embark on an awesome ATV ride that takes you up the rugged terrain for a thrilling experience.

As you descend the majestic mountain, you'll make your way to the vibrant valley city of Anum-Asamankese, where the affable locals warmly welcome you.

For those seeking the answers to Africa's painful past, a visit to the historic Assin Manso Slave River Site will leave you reflective. It was here that enslaved men, women, sons, and daughters took their last bath before beginning their barefoot trek to the Cape Coast and El Mina Slave Dungeons. Walk in their footsteps as you learn of their agonizing journey, and pay homage to the first enslaved ancestors who returned home through the Door of Return. The stories of Lady Crystal from Jamaica and Carson from New York will inspire you as you honor their legacy each year on August 1st.

The river's cool waters serve as a reminder of the anguish endured, and the Wall of Return allows you to sign your name for a small fee that goes toward maintaining the site.

Ampesi

Popular Food:
Ampesi—boiled yam, plantain, and cassava

Destination: Aburi Mountains, Accra, Anum-Asamankese

B is for Beaches

(mpoano ahorow)

Be sure to stop by the beautiful beaches of Accra like Labadi Beach or Liberty. The Prampram Beach is just a few tro-tro rides and about 45 minutes outside Accra. Have time? Travel inland to the shores of Cape Coast to soak up the sun.

If you're like me when it comes to travel, getting your hair 'slayed' is in the top 5 of your pre departure plans. But, when traveling to Ghana, I implore you to wait and experience African hair braiders! Not only is the process of up to 4-5 expert braiders cool (and pain free if you're tender-headed like me), but it's inexpensive, too. You can get a wash and braided style with hair extensions –services that could easily be $200-300 USD—for less than $60!

The beautiful Botanical Gardens of the Aburi Mountains is a must see for those looking to take in nature. The Botanical Gardens not only captures trees and flowers from Ghana, but also blossoms gifted from other Countries, like China. The gardens will make for some of the best photo backdrops.

Bliss is a brand-new bowling and bouncing trampoline entertainment center in Accra. It boasts a beautifully designed bar, an arcade with VR games, and an outdoor teacup twirl ride.

Banku

Popular Food:
Banku—fermented maize and cassava dough served with soup, okra stew or a pepper sauce with fish

Destination: Botanical Gardens (Aburi, Ghana); Bloom Bar (Accra)

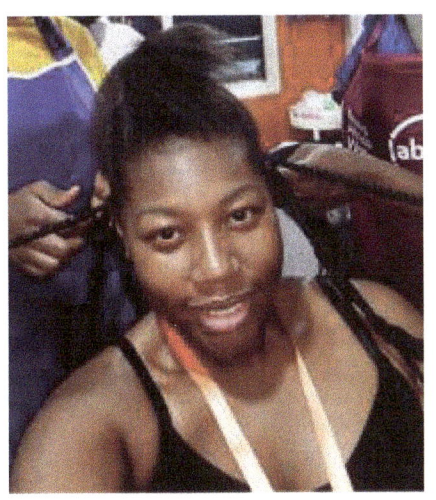

C is for Cedi

You cannot spend in Ghana without checking out their currency--the Cedi, which features the Big 6! The Big 6 were the leaders of the Gold Coast Convention before Ghana received her independence. They are considered Ghana's founding fathers.

Let's change topics and see what culinary snacks we can consume while visiting Ghana. Cocoa is one of Ghana's most valuable natural resources. Ghana produces about 50% of the world's cocoa along with the Ivory Coast! Chocolate tasting? Don't mind if I do. A newly emerging sector for capitalizing currency is cashew mining. Now, if you are still on the beaches drinking coconut water and eating cassava, don't forget to indulge in the array of street snacks: crispy chips, crunchy crackers, or creamy coconut candies.

If you find yourself in Cape Coast, make sure to swing by the university and the castles, also known as the slave dungeons. Step into the place where enslaved Africans were held for months before being transported to the shores of America. The term "castle" describes the structure of the edifice, but "dungeon" captures the essence of its purpose.

Chocolate

Popular Food:
Chocolate, cassava, cashews

Destination: Cape Coast Castles (Central region)

D is for Door of No Return
(ɔPon a wontumi nsan nkɔ hɔ bio)

The Door of No Return is a definite historical landmark to see while in Ghana. Travel to Cape Coast to visit the slave dungeons, where once free Africans were detained, deprived and subjected to the darkest deprivations for months. Be prepared that this may be a deeply emotional and teary visit. As we dry our tears and depart the dungeons through the Door of Return, we listen to the distinct call of Africa: the drums that have long directed and driven our ancestors. Be sure to take a drum and dance class while in Ghana. You can look for classes at the Abajo Café at the Arts Center in Accra.

The Divine 9 is a distinguished collective of Black Greek Lettered Organizations (BGLOs): Alpha Phi Alpha Fraternity, Inc., Alpha Kappa Alpha Sorority, Inc., Omega Psi Phi Fraternity, Inc., Kappa Alpha Psi Fraternity, Inc., Delta Sigma Theta Sorority, Inc., Phi Beta Sigma Fraternity, Inc., Zeta Phi Beta Sorority, Inc., Sigma Gamma Rho Sorority, Inc., and Iota Phi Theta Fraternity, Inc. These BGLOs were founded in the early 1900s when many other sororities and fraternities on college campuses—created to foster community and networking among students—excluded individuals based on income, gender, and most blatantly, race. Black collegiates were systematically denied access to these organizations. With the establishment of Historically Black Colleges and Universities (HBCUs) through funds from the Freedmen's Bureau, BGLOs soon followed, driven by a commitment to empower Black students, build enduring legacies, and dismantle barriers rooted in systemic oppression.

Rooted in the rhythm of the motherland, BGLOs honor African traditions through step shows, chants, and synchronized performances—offering a unique and unmatched cultural expression. Step, a powerful art form blending precision, unity, and call-and-response, serves as a cultural bridge that connects the past with the present. These vibrant displays of solidarity not only celebrate African heritage but also embody the spirit of perseverance and community that continues to uplift Black culture worldwide.

Domedo

Popular Food:
Domedo—spicy beef or goat stew

Destination: Door of No Return (Central region)

E is for Estuary

(asubɔnten no ano)

An estuary is a partially enclosed, coastal water body where freshwater meets the salty embrace of the ocean. A boat ride from the Aqua Safari Resort in Ada, Ghana, offers the perfect opportunity to explore the ethereal Ada Estuary: where the mighty Volta Lake flows into the vast Atlantic Ocean. The Aqua Safari resort is exactly the escape you need if you like private bungalows, horseback riding, beautiful aquariums, water sports, and the luxury of pool-side views with bar service.

Another eye-catching sight to behold is the 'Eka' adornment worn by chiefs on their right hand as a symbol of their elevated position. In Ghana, elders are esteemed and treated with the utmost respect. Women older than you may be affectionately called "Aunty," while men may be addressed as "Father"—a reflection of the deep reverence for senior members of the community.

Ghana is full of entrepreneurs hustling on every corner. From women selling boiled eggs (a favorite of Reggie), plantains, and peanuts to men peddling shoe polish, gum and electronics, you'll find everything you need (and even some things you didn't know you needed) right at your fingertips. The streets are lined with these enterprising individuals, each offering a piece of their entrepreneurial spirit. Elephant tusks, once traded for ivory, were sought after by Europeans during Ghana's colonial past. El Mina, as the Portuguese named it, speaks to the historic abundance of gold and resources in the region, a name that still resonates today.

Egusi

Popular Food:
Egusi—boiled yam, plantain, and cassava

Destination: Elmina, Ghana (Central region); Estuary of Ada (Accra region)

F is for Fugu

Fugu (not Fubu) is a fabric that is faithfully handwoven with origins in Northern Ghana. It's a fashionable, striped and stylish garment worn by men and women, often paired with fabulous matching hats. Fugu is also known as Batakari or Smock. This fine fabric pairs effortlessly with your favorite pair of jeans for a fun and casual look or can be dressed up with slacks or a skirt to show a formal, professional appearance.

Functionally, you may need to find your way to a Forex Bureau—no, no, not for day trading on the stock market, but to facilitate the exchange of money for local cedi. Fast tip: Bring $100 bills, as they are exchanged at a favorable rate compared to smaller denominations.

Fried fish and fried pork were two of my faves to enjoy. For some flavorful, fiery African eats, stop by the Freetown Chophouse to feast on food and the delicacies from Sierra Leone! Funerals are a festive affair in Ghana, where people come from near and far to pay their respects by dancing the 'fontom fom' to celebrate life.

Forts are another fascinating feature of Ghana. The country holds the foremost position in Africa for having the most forts constructed during colonial times, when it was subjected to the harsh and relentless forces of enslavement. Many of these forts changed hands due to rivalries and conflicts among various colonial powers vying for control. Fetish priests played a significant role in Ghanaian life in the past. If you find yourself in Kumasi, you may want to explore the history and stories related to these spiritual figures.

For refreshing indulgence, I scream, you scream, we all scream for ice cream. Try Fan frozen treats, which come in a variety of irresistible flavors: FanChoco, FanYogo, and FanIce. What's your flavor?

fufu

Popular Food:
Fufu—boiled yam, plantain, and cassava

Destination: Fort William, Region: Central. Freetown Chophouse (Sierra Leone cuisine) Region: Greater Accra

R.I.P

G is for Gold (sika kↄkↄↄ)

Ghana, formerly glorified as the Gold Coast by European colonizers, gained its name from the abundance of this glittering natural resource. Generations of colonizers have journeyed to Ghana in search of its gleaming gold. Today, you can get gorgeous custom-made jewelry from local jewelers. Many countries, like China, are still exploiting the country by setting up gold mining using only Chinese laborers, and not contributing back to Ghana's economy.

Ghana was gifted its modern name in honor of a grand medieval West African empire, now situated in parts of modern-day Mali Senegal, neighboring nations. Ghana is divided into 16 geographical regions, with Accra as its growing and bustling capital city. Accra is in the Greater Accra region, glistening along the southeastern shoreline of the nation.

Ghana is graced with a variety of ethnic groups. One of the largest groups is the Ga people, also known as the Ga-Adangme, which includes almost 10 other smaller groups. The Ga people are found in the capital city of Accra and gathered in parts of the Eastern region of Ghana. They also have a global presence in neighboring West African countries like Togo and Benin.

The Ghana Must Go bag is an iconic, unmistakable symbol of travel, resilience, and practicality. These woven plastic bags, known for their bold and colorful plaid patterns, are the MVPs of packing-- carrying everything from clothes to household items and even dreams--even a WHOLE HOUSE! Despite their origins tied to a complex history (ask a Ghanaian or Nigerian about that!), they've become a continental African identity. Affordable, durable, and unapologetically functional, a GMG bag is a must-have companion for any journey. Need to move your whole life in one go? Grab a Ghana Must Go bag—it's a vibe, not just a bag!

Garri

Popular Food:
Garri - ground cassava used to make dishes like eba

Destination: Ghana Forts (multiple cities)

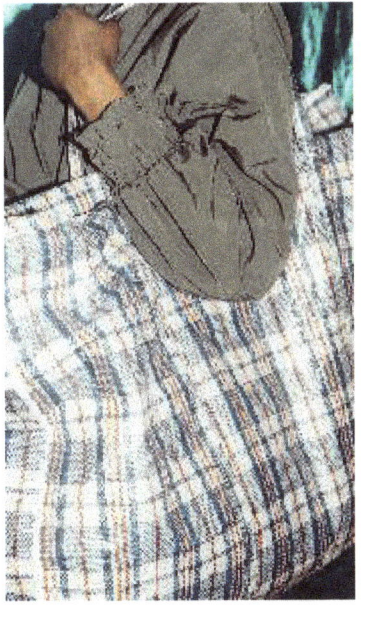

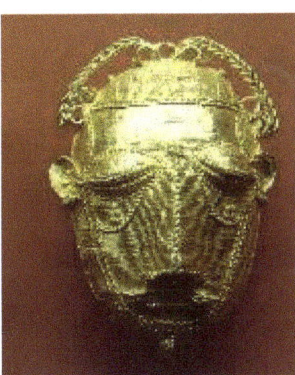

H is for Hotel

(ahɔhobea)

How will you be hosted while in Ghana? Your housing options are happily plentiful: hotels, hostels, or homes for rent are all available to you. However, no matter where you rest your head, it's worth heading out to hunt for historic and modern architecture. You'll notice hints of European influence in newer building designs compared to the handcrafted, traditional structures that define Ghanaian culture. For a heartfelt experience, hop in a car and travel about two hours outside Accra to visit the Tamatoku community in Ada, where you can see traditional living up close.

Hotdogs—for breakfast? Yes, while in Ghana, you may notice hotels and hostels serving two familiar foods in an unexpected hybrid: hotdogs and beans, paired with eggs and veggies. Don't expect the sweet, saucy beans from home—these beans are healthier, without the heavy helpings of brown sugar, ketchup or barbecue sauce typical in the U.S. Instead, they're hearty, making for a uniquely Ghanaian morning meal. Mix them together if you like, but let your palate enjoy the harmonious flavor of this local twist!

Home-Cooked Meals > eating out. In America, highways are lined with eateries, and families pack into restaurants to share meals. But in Ghana, there's nothing quite like the warmth of home-cooked meals. Whether you're in the heart of Accra or nestled in the countryside, food brings people together like nothing else. In the busy streets, you'll find vendors selling jollof rice with fried plantains and fufu with light soup—true tastes of tradition. Yet, it's in villages like those near Ada where the real magic happens. Here, meals are lovingly prepared from local ingredients, often passed down through generations. Haako, a hearty millet porridge, is a popular breakfast, providing both comfort and nourishment. Families gather around offering these homemade dishes, with a healthy dose of Ghanaian hospitality.

Haako

Popular Food:
Haako—millet porridge

Destination: **Ho, Ghana (Volta region)**

I is for Independence

(ahofadi wonya)

Independence! Ghana made incredible history as the first sub-Saharan nation to gain freedom from colonial rule. Under the inspiring leadership of its first prime minister and president, Kwame Nkrumah, Ghana achieved independence in 1957. Celebrate this momentous occasion by visiting Independence Square, also known as Black Star Square, on March 6 for the impressive Independence Day festivities. While you're there, don't miss the inviting Independence Beach—just bring your swim gear and enjoy some invigorating fun in the sun. Instruments inspire intricate impressions, with carved engravings and crafted creations capturing Ghana's musical heritage.

Intricate instrument engravings infuse insight into Ghana's musical traditions, blending art and acoustics in harmonious harmony. Illustrated instruments invoke imagination, immortalizing the melodies of Ghana's rich rhythms through art and craftsmanship.

Indecision is always a part of travel. "What should I bring to Ghana?" Packing for Ghana requires careful planning. Use all of your international luggage allowance—two checked bags, a carry-on, and a personal item. Essential items include luggage locks, detergent sheets for laundry, bug spray with 10% DEET, sunblock, and a Type-G power converter. Don't forget to pack all your prescription medications first! Download WhatsApp so that you can keep in contact with your family and friends back home, as well as communicate with locals. For a trip as enriching as Ghana, preparation is key to enjoying every moment of your journey.

Itso

Popular Food:
Itso—palm nut soup with fish or other meat

Destination: Independence Square (Greater Accra region)

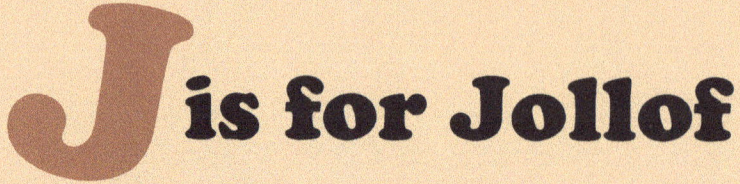 J is for Jollof

Jollof rice: let the jabs and jests begin! One thing to expect on the African continent is the jollof rice wars. Every country claims the crown for cooking the best bowl–so grab a spoon and join the juicy debate! In Ghana, the jollof is spiced to perfection, simmered in savory tomato sauce, and paired with fried plantains, grilled chicken or even goat meat. Whether served at a street-side stall or a festive gathering, Ghanaian jollof deserves its joyful reputation. So, what's your judgment? Can Ghana's jollof claim the top spot?

Ghana is famed for its jubilant bead-making traditions, and markets across the country showcase stunning handcrafted jewelry. From tiny translucent beads to bold, brightly colored ones, each piece tells a story. In towns like Krobo, artisans craft these treasures using age-old techniques passed down through generations. These jewels aren't just accessories—they hold cultural and spiritual significance, often worn during rites of passage, festivals and weddings.

Waist beads, in particular, carry deep meaning in Ghanaian culture. Traditionally, they are worn by women and hidden beneath clothing, intended only for their husband to see in the privacy of the home—adding an element of intimacy and sensuality to a relationship. However, as waist beads have gained popularity in America, their use has taken on entirely new meanings. Many women now wear them as a form of weight-loss tracking, where the beads tighten or loosen with changes in body shape. Others, including men (particularly in the LGBTQ+ community), brandish them as fashion statements, pairing them with halter tops and crop tops. While this trend celebrates the beauty of the beads, it is a departure from their cultural roots, which value modesty and personal significance over public display. If you spot a stall adorned with strings of sparkling beads during your travels, don't hesitate to join the fun and pick out a piece of Ghana to take home—just remember to honor its traditions and origins.

The Jubilee House gleams in its jubilant golden glory, a jewel of Accra's jaw-dropping architecture. Located along Liberation Road, this jewel of a presidential palace was originally constructed by the British Gold Coast Government before Ghana's jubilant independence in 1957. Once known as the Flagstaff House, it was renamed Jubilee House by President Nana Addo Danquah Akuffo Addo in 2018. Whether you journey inside or not, its majestic structure is worth a visit. Trust me—you'll catch glimpses of this jaw-dropping landmark as you jaunt between Legon, Osu, and downtown Accra.

Jollof Rice

Popular Food:
Jollof—spiced rice cooked in tomato sauce

Destination: Jirapa (Upper West region)

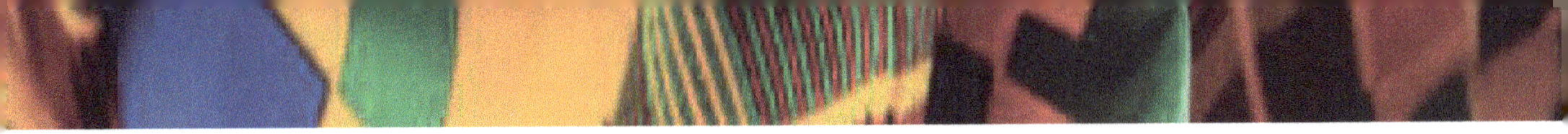

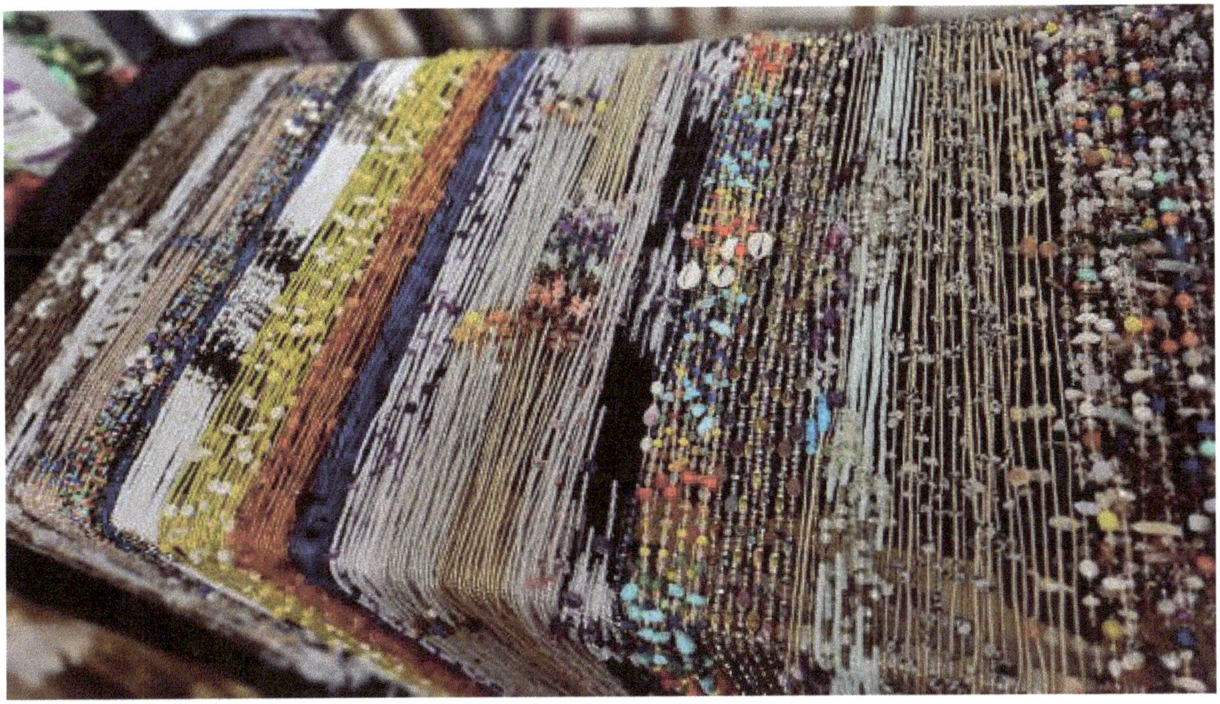

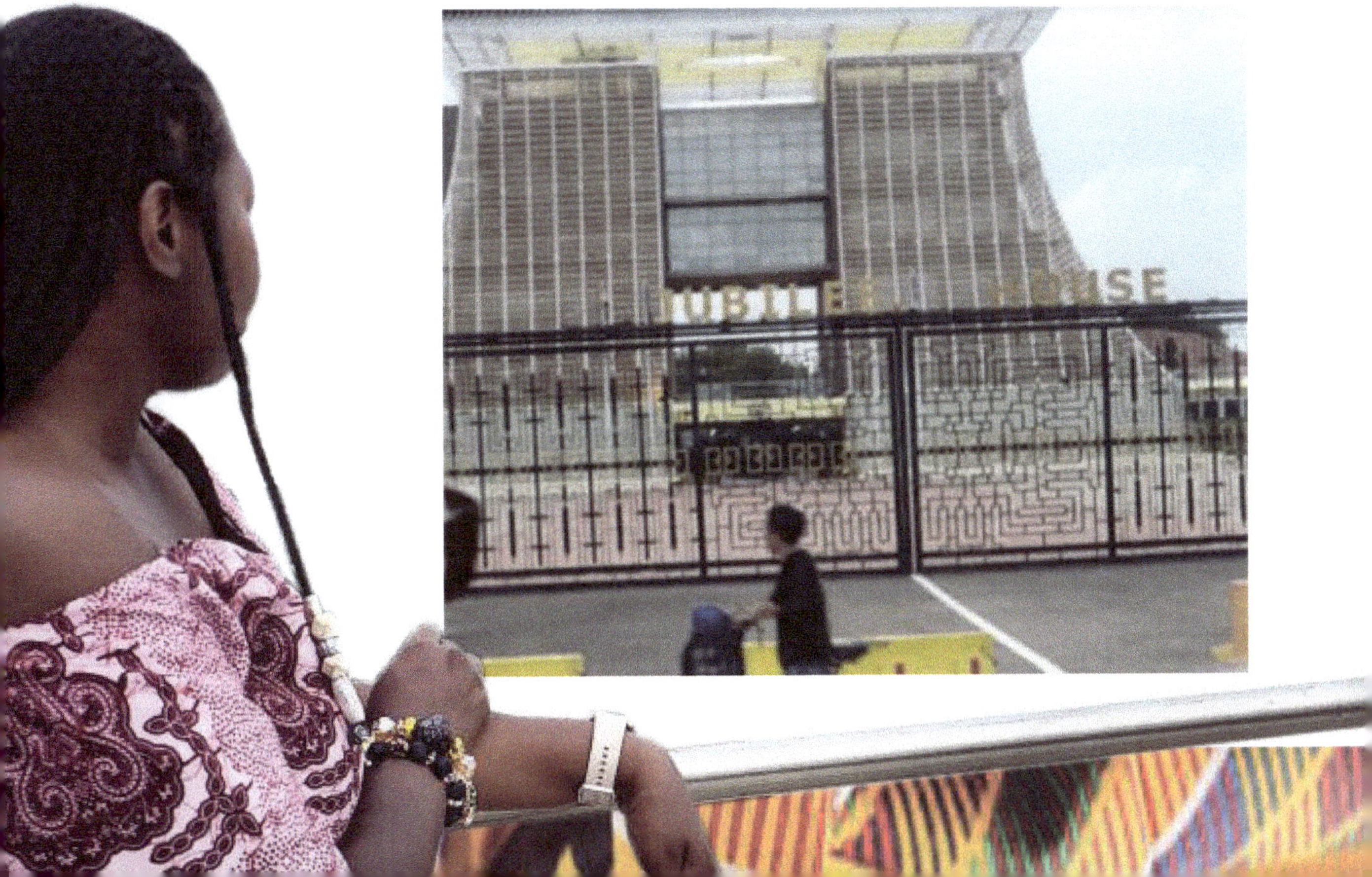

K is for Kwame Nkrumah

Kwame Nkrumah (member of Phi Beta Sigma Fraternity, Inc., my constitutionally bound brother as a member of Zeta Phi Beta Sorority, Inc.) is the key figure in Ghana's fight for independence, the king of the country's liberation from British colonial rule. As the pioneer of Ghana's path to freedom and its first president, his monumental impact makes him a legendary leader worthy of his own page.

Keep your eyes peeled for Kwame Nkrumah's legacy across the country, from the Kwame Nkrumah Memorial Center in Accra to the Kwame Nkrumah University of Science and Technology (KNUST) in Kumasi, both standing as lasting landmarks of his influence. His likeness and legacy all grace the Ghanaian cedi, with his image proudly placed among "The Big 6."

In addition to his monumental legacy, Kwame Nkrumah's daughter, Samia Yaba Christina Nkrumah, also plays an important role in the Zeta Phi Beta Sorority, Inc. Samia was inducted as an honorary member in 2022, making her the Soror of every member of Zeta. Her induction, alongside American actress and philanthropist Dawnn Lewis, solidified a legacy of leadership and service that runs deep in the Nkrumah family. I had the honor of meeting Samia during my initial trip to Ghana during the summer of 2022—an honor–meeting the honorable Kwame Nkrumah's daughter–yet, not knowing I was taking a picture with my soon- to-be Soror!

How many Kwame Nkrumah tributes did you encounter during your journey? Whether in statues, signageor on currency, his contributions continue to keep the country moving forward.

Kebob

Popular Food:
Kebob— spiced up grilled meat on sticks

Destination: Kwame Nkurumah Memorial Center
(Greater Accra region)

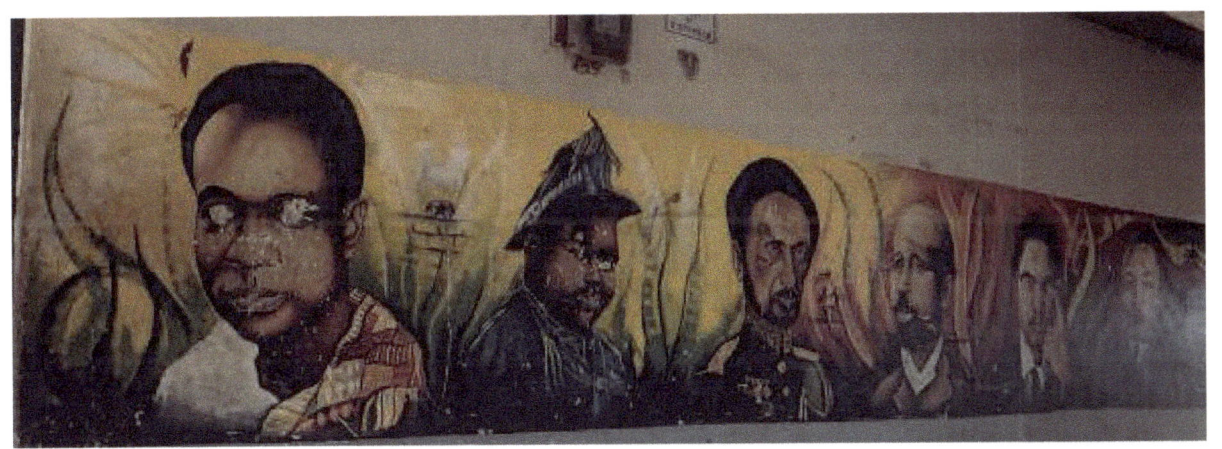

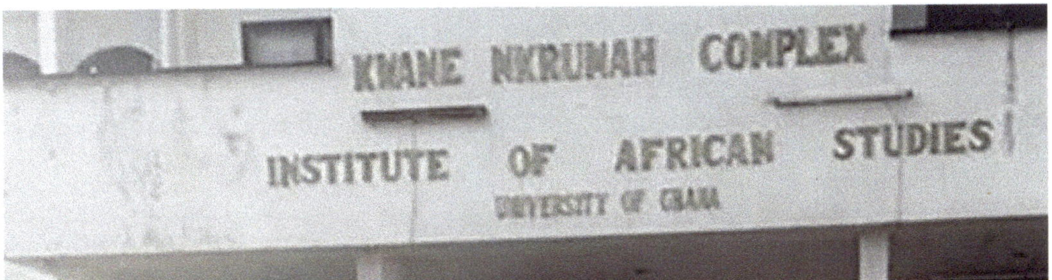
KWAME NKRUMAH COMPLEX
INSTITUTE OF AFRICAN STUDIES
UNIVERSITY OF GHANA

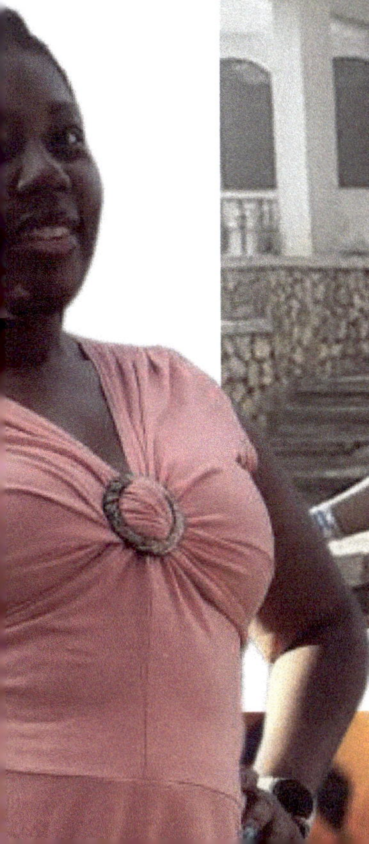

K is for Kotoka Airport

Kicking off your Ghanaian adventure, Kotoka International Airport (KIA) is likely your first stop on this life-changing journey. Though smaller than global giants like Washington D.C.'s Dulles International Airport or Atlanta's Hartsfield-Jackson, KIA operates with keen efficiency.

One key tip: KEEP YOUR LUGGAGE TAGS ON ARRIVAL! In my travels across four continents, KIA is the only airport where baggage tags are checked before you exit–a clever security measure that I deeply appreciate.

Kumasi, a city located in the heart of the Ashanti region, is a place where culture and commerce collide. Known for its colossal Ketejia Market, Kumasi is a kaleidoscope of colors, sounds and bargains. This bustling market is the perfect spot for shopping and engaging in the art of bartering. As the home of the Asante tribe, Kumasi's history runs deep—though it is often mispronounced as "Ashanti" by the British, the name actually means "because of wars."

As you navigate through Ghana, don't miss trying local treats like kabobs, which can be made with meats like chicken or goat, kenkey— chilled fermented corn dumpling, kube cake (a sweet coconut dessert), and kelewele (spicy fried plantains with peanuts). For those who love a little kick in their food, kelewele is heavy on the heat, a familiar note in many West African dishes. For dessert, kube cake is a treat worth the extra steps to work off as you groove to the rhythm of the kpalogo (/pa/lah/go) drum.

Kelewele

Popular Food:
Kelewele— spicy fried plantains with peanuts

Destination: **Kakum National Park (central region)**

KOTOKA INTERNATIONAL AIRPORT

L is for Linda Dor

When traveling between Kumasi and Accra, you must stop to lounge a bit at the Linda Dor Highway Rest Stop. It is sooo massive! Make sure you have some small cash to pay to use the restroom and grab snacks. Another landmark you'll find in Accra is the famous "I ❤ Accra" artwork, located in the Osu district. A colorful symbol of Ghana's capital, this vibrant spot is perfect for photos and offers a fun way to showcase your journey. It's a true reflection of Accra's energy –welcoming, lively, and full of life.

Just a short trip from there, you'll encounter historical Larabanga Mosque in the Savannah region, a landmark that represents Ghana's spiritual and architectural heritage. For nature lovers, Lake Volta, one of the largest artificial lakes in the world, offers a breathtaking retreat with stunning views. Boat rides on the lake, coupled with the peaceful landscape, create a serene experience that will leave you refreshed.

If you're craving more adventure, head to the Cape Coast Adventure Park. This destination offers thrilling activities, including zip-lining, a canopy walk (with the "rickety" bridge experience!), and other exciting outdoor sports. It's a great place to add a little adrenaline to your trip while still soaking in the beauty of the surroundings.

Lastly, I had the honor of experiencing libation ceremonies during my trip. It was my first time participating in these deeply meaningful and spiritual traditions. Whether by water or alcohol, these ceremonies help connect participants with the Creator and leave you with a profound sense of reverence.

Lonto

Popular Food:
Lonto— fermented corn dough used to make dishes like kenkey or banku

Destination: Larabanga Mosque (Savannah region)

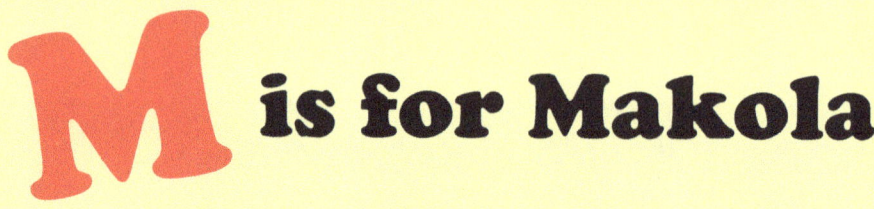 **M is for Makola**

Mmmm, where to start—should we marvel at the magnificent mountains that decorate the landscape across Ghana? Whether you're winding through the hills or enjoying the rolling terrain, the country's natural beauty will leave you in awe.

Now, let's go shopping at the bustling Makola Market in Accra. This is the marketplace where you'll find mounds of textiles, where masterful seamstresses and tailors will make beautiful, custom-made pieces just for you. From mouth-watering spices that pack a punch, to bags, toys, and even local food, this place is a sensory meltdown. But beware: markups on the horizon! The locals might charge Americans a little more, assuming we have money to burn. It's often best to go with a local guide who can help you shop at the local rate for more manageable prices.

If you're in need of a mellow treat, be sure to try Milo by Nestlé. For hot chocolate lovers, this is the perfect beverage to sip on, offering a comforting blend of chocolatey goodness to enjoy anytime. Make sure you don't miss the magnificent Manhyia Palace in Kumasi, the royal residence of the Asantehene. This majestic palace is a museum rich with mystical history and memories of the Ashanti kingdom. Learn about the mighty king and his kingdom's magnificent heritage.

And for those seeking a majestic adventure, don't forget about Mole National Park in the Northern region. With its miles of manicured nature, wild mammals like elephants roam free. A safari here will give you a magnificent view of Ghana's marvelous wildlife and a chance to meet the animals that live in this expansive park.

Moi Moi

Popular Food:

Moi moi—steamed bean pudding (similar to refried beans)

Destination: **Mole National Park (Northern region)**

N is for Neem

Navigating through Ghana, you'll find the neem tree a natural remedy for many ailments. Nurture your health with neem leaves, which are used to brew a refreshing tea with lime—perfect for purging your system of toxins.

Need something for your teeth? Neem stems, though notoriously bitter, make an effective brush. Now, let me be real with you—when I first traveled to Ghana, I contracted Covid (yep, it happened). Yet, I was encouraged to nurture myself with steaming cups of neem tea, taken under a blanket, and consumed 3-4 cups a day. I won't sugarcoat it—it was nasty. N-A-S-T-Y! The taste? I describe it as a bitter blend of household cleaners and, well, a pinch of death, but hey, I recovered in just 3 days with no residual side effects. Now, I'm a believer. Next time I travel, I'll happily sip it for general purification. Neem's no-nonsense nature cleanses both body and soul!

Next, for a sweet treat, try Nkatie cake, a Ghanaian delight similar to what Americans call peanut brittle. Named kongodo in Guinea and louga in Senegal, this nutty snack is perfect for anyone with a sweet tooth. If you're nuts for peanuts, this delicious delicacy is for you!

Nungua, a notable coastal town, is known for its rich fishing heritage and the annual Homowo festival celebrated by the Ga people. Homowo marks the end of famine, with the sprinkling of the traditional dish, kpokpoi, to bless the land and nurture abundance. The noble people of Nungua also honor their ancestors through this meaningful celebration.

Nkatie Cake

Popular Food:
Nkatie cake — peanut brittle

Destination: Navrongo (Upper East region, Burkina Faso border)

O is for Obama Kente

O is for Obama Kente cloth. Kente cloth is a one-of-a-kind woven fabric worn by the Akan tribe. Often we associate women with the textile market; however, if you go to the Bonwire Tourist Centre in Ejisu, Kumasi, you'll observe that the ornate kente is mostly made by young boys! Single, double, or triple weave patterns are organized together to create patterns for remembering special or outstanding moments, with each pattern and color selection carrying a unique meaning. As the first American president of African descent, Barack Obama's election was an overwhelming victory for diasporans worldwide. Ghanaian people adorned President Obama with what is now known as the "Obama Kente." Its opulent colors and intricate patterns represent diversity and richness of African heritage, while the cloth itself can be symbolic of achievements of African Americans.

Out on the town? I know you'll want to experience Ghana's outstanding nightlife and restaurants. Be sure to grab a taxi and head to the Osu district! There, you'll find not only open roof top clubs–providing great optics for your photos, but also street vendors to barter with and restaurants that stay open late.

O is also for okra. Now, you know we Americans live for batter fried everything...but if you are open to immerse yourself in authentic Ghanaian food culture, you must try okra stew. It varies from popular New Orleans gumbo where okra takes a one-note supporting ingredient. In this thick, soupy traditional dish cooked in a large metal pot over an open flame, okra is the star. I had the opportunity to watch women in a local village make okra stew from scratch during a community service project put on by the D4 Collective (Alpha Kappa Alpha, Delta Sigma Theta, Zeta Phi Beta, and Sigma Gamma Rho Black Greek Lettered Organizations), which operates frequently in service and fellowship in Accra.

Omo Tuo

Popular Food:
Omo tuo—rice balls served with soup or stew

Destination: **Osu (Greater Accra region)**

P is for Peduase

Pondering your journey through the picturesque Aburi Mountains? Pause and peer out for the Peduase Lodge, a pristine place built by Ghana's first president, Kwame Nkrumah, as a peaceful summer residence. This palace in the town of Peduase (close to Kitase) offers a panoramic view of the surrounding peaks. While the Peduase Lodge now plays host to state guests, you can still enjoy the nearby Peduase Valley Resort. I personally spent a fun-filled day there with my 11-year-old son, and let me tell you, it's a family paradise! With a plentiful buffet, a pool, basketball courts, trampoline park, slides and swings for the kiddos, a petting zoo, an ostrich farm, massage parlor, and gym, this place packs a punch for family fun. It's definitely a must-stay, where something for everyone awaits!

Pesewa for your thoughts? Okay, okay—let's call it a penny for your thoughts, but Ghana's coins are called pesewas, in denominations of 0.01, 0.05, 0.1, 0.2, 0.5, and 1.0. So, count those pesewas and take a trip to Parliament!

Parliament building in Accra, is a beautiful and colorful premise that stands out amidst the city's landscape. You can watch proceedings from the public gallery during the week. I had the honor of sitting in on two Parliamentary sessions, and it was a fascinating moment! It was eye-opening to witness the perfect fusion of European-style government with Ghanaian traditions.

Part of the fascinating sights is witnessing Western suits side by side with traditional attire, such as the Fugu, was powerful. I even observed the Bible being referenced for debates, and the rise and fall of the MPs' voices as they passionately debated important issues. It was a unique and powerful cultural encounter.

Peanut Soup

Popular Food:

*Peanut nut soup—made from a peanut butter base, with tomatoes and chillies *spicy***

Destination: **Peduase Valley Resort (Aburi Mountains, Greater, Accra region)**

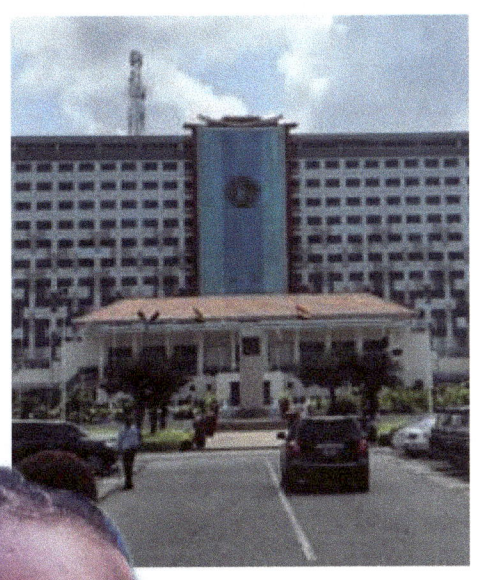

is for Queen Mother

In Ghana, certain powerful women are revered as Queen Mothers—influential figures who serve as the female counterpart to the chief. Their titles and roles depend on the significance of their 'enstoolment' (installation), and each title is indicative of her leadership position. For instance, the Queen Mother for the development of a city might bear the title Nkosuohemaa. These women hold strong spiritual, political, and cultural influence, shaping the future of their communities.

In Kumasi (Asante Region), you'll find the Queen's Palace, a historic site deeply linked to the Asante royal family and their heritage. The palace serves as a center of tradition and governance for the Asanti people, where the Queen Mother holds a significant role in overseeing cultural and administrative matters. Just nearby, the Quarters of the Royal Asante is a testament to the enduring influence of the Queen Mother in shaping the kingdom's leadership. Here, the Queen Mother plays a vital part in guiding the community, blending both authority and wisdom as she upholds the values of the Ashanti people.

Speaking of quality leadership, quality education is another priority for Ghana. The country continues to strive for improvements in its educational system, with a focus on providing equitable access to quality schooling, especially for girls and marginalized groups. One standout Queen Mother, Nana Akosua Serwaa Se3oyo I, is making waves at Academic City College in Accra, where she's leading a charge for academic excellence and greater opportunities for young people.

Quail Eggs

Popular Food:
Quail eggs—used in various dishes

Destination: Queen's Palace, Kumasi (Asante region)

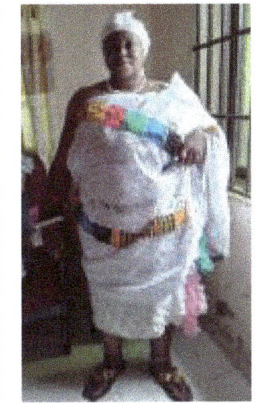

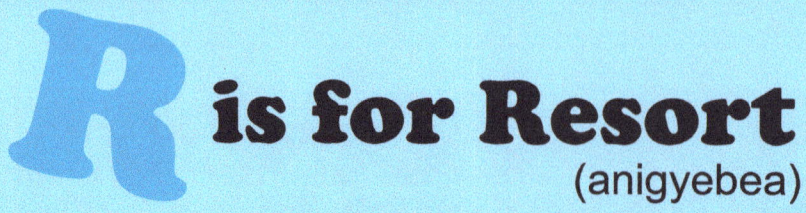 R is for Resort
(anigyebea)

In Ghana, rivers run through the landscape, and one of the best ways to experience them is by taking a relaxing boat ride from Aqua Safari Resort along the Volta River. It's a perfect way to rest and refresh while taking in the scenic beauty of the area. For dinner, red snapper is a reliable choice, often served alongside banku, a staple Ghanaian dish. But be warned – Ghanaian food can be remarkably raging in spice. If you're like me and a bit of a recluse when it comes to hot food, don't forget to request your dishes with reduced "pe-puh" (pepper). Trust me, this isn't your typical run-of-the-mill black pepper, but more of a robust and fiery sensation.

When it comes to roundabouts, there's a random rule of the road in Ghana. Unlike in many other countries where cars follow a smooth, single-file procession, Ghana's roundabouts can feel like recently dropped puzzle pieces, cars crammed together in a chaotic yet somehow routinely efficient way. Be ready for the ride of your life as you navigate them!

Religion in Ghana is a reverent part of daily life. The country is home to a rich diversity of faiths, including Christianity, Islam, and traditional African religions. Whether you find yourself stepping into a grand Protestant cathedral or a serene Muslim mosque, the religious devotion of the people is palpable. As you roam through cities and towns, you may also come across synagogues or smaller temples, each offering a window into the unique religious experiences and rituals of the communities. From the rhythmic chants in churches to the peaceful call to prayer, Ghana's spiritual landscape is rich with history, and witnessing these religious practices will leave you with a sense of respect and admiration for the people's deep-rooted faith.

Lastly, remember a respectful rule of conduct in Ghana: always use your right hand when giving or receiving items. Whether it's a refreshing beverage, paying for a service, or simply waving, the right hand is a symbol of respect. Using your left hand is often considered disrespectful in Ghanaian culture, so make sure to be mindful of thissmall but important social norm

Red Red

Popular Food:

Red-red—(spicy)fried plantains and beans stew

Destination: **Rawlings Park (Greater Accra region)**

S is for Shea Butter

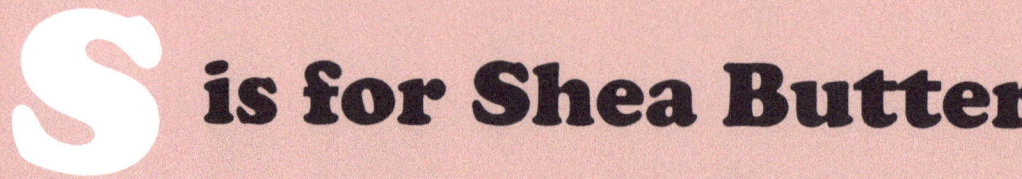

Shea butter is one of the world's most popular natural moisturizers and it is one of Ghana's top exports. Shea butter is made from the nuts found in abundance on trees in the Northern Region. Traditionally produced by women, this precious product is a symbol of empowerment for Ghanaian women entrepreneurs. So when you purchase authentic Ghanaian shea butter, you're not just nourishing your skin, you're supporting powerful women making their mark in the world! "Who run the world? Girls!" #BlackWomenRock!

Speaking of empowerment, one thing you absolutely must do when you land in Ghana is secure a skilled seamstress to take your measurements. Prepare for stylish, sophisticated, and stunning custom-made clothing that's as unique as your journey. My personal seamstress, Jane M of Mejane Fashion Designer, is exceptional at her craft. You can check out her incredible work on her Instagram page Mejane Fashion Designer. Watching her measure my son for his first tailored outfit was a touching experience. The moment you don your sensational, sleek new outfits back home, you'll be the talk of the town. You'll find these new pieces are the perfect conversation starters, inviting you to sew a story with style about the unforgettable travel experiences, forever reminders of the Ghanaian spirit, sophistication, and splendor.

While you're exploring Ghana, you're bound to notice supersized snails crawling along the ground, especially during the rainy season. These enormous snails are not just a sight to behold—they're also a delicacy! Ghanaians prepare snails in a variety of ways, from roasting to adding them to soups. Some say they have a unique flavor and are quite nutritious, packed with protein. If you're feeling adventurous, consider sampling this sizable snack during your trip. It's a seasonal specialty you won't forget!

In Ghanaian tradition, when friends are dining together, each person orders an entrée and shares it among the table, creating a warm and sociable setting that fosters connection and camaraderie. This communal style of eating reminds me of my experience in China, where dishes are also passed around and shared. Savor the flavor of traditional cuisine by sampling a spread of savory selections like shito—a spicy black pepper sauce that adds a fiery kick to rice, fish, or meat dishes. Pair it with other local favorites, like samosas, and you'll experience the symphony of spices that define Ghanaian cooking. But consider yourself warned—Ghanaian food isn't for the faint of heart when it comes to spice! The sheer selection of seasonings, from smoky scents to sharp, sizzling spices, will dazzle your senses and add depth to every dish. Whether you're enjoying a bowl of tuo zaafi or savoring grilled red snapper, every bite is a flavorful adventure.

Shito Sauce

Popular Food:

Shito– a spicy black pepper sauce to pour over meat or rice

Destination: **Sunyami, Region: Brong Ahafo (Burkina Faso border)**
Skybar (dinner night life) Region: Greater Accra

T is for Tro-Tro

A tro-tro trip must be taken at least once in Accra to travel to towns or nearby cities. In a slightly tattered transport, a tro-tro ride is a local transportation treasure, functioning as a hybrid taxi, transit bus and a shared Uber all in one. For a drive that would cost at least 100 cedis in a private automobile, you can travel to Prampram beach for as low as 40 cedis.

There are other local travel transportation options to consider during your stay. My son, Reggie, and I trekked to the town of Cape Coast, using the "big red" VIP bus. If you've ever read Clifford the Big Red Dog, imagine this bus as the grown-up version—bright red, massive, and reliable! The VIP bus even had a free Fruit Ninja-type game in the headrest to keep my son entertained throughout the journey. Just like Greyhound, the trip includes a few restroom stops along the way. On the return to Accra, we opted for InterCity STC Coaches Ltd., another popular transportation option. However, this ride lacked the tantalizing touches, bells and whistles of the VIP bus. Without any entertainment to offer, it's fair to compare InterCity STC to the "Spirit Airlines" of Ghana's bus services—functional but totally tame. Still, both options are cost-effective and efficient for touring towns and traversing terrain in Ghana's tropical treasures.

The Ghanaian business industry is booming with textiles. At the Makola Market, tucked in the heart of Accra, you may barter for your preferred fabric or order custom textiles tailored by a kente manufacturer near Kumasi, if you've traveled inland. Six yards is typically enough to make a top and a bottom for both men and women. Three yards should be enough to have just a top made. Many organizations even have fabrics adorned with special text or logos, which can be turned into the garment of choice.

The annual Taste of Ghana festival is the greatest place to swiftly immerse yourself in the top-tier treasures of Ghanaian culture, from food, to art and cinematography, tailored trends, and more. This celebration is held in December in Black Star Square (Independence Square) in Accra, the country's capital.

Tuo Zaafi

Popular Food:

Tuo zaafi—millet or corn dough that can be eaten with soup

Destination: Tamale (Northern region) (tama means "shea fruit")

U is for University

However you choose to get around, unlock unique opportunities to spot universities like the unmistakable University of Ghana. It boasts an uncanny teaching hospital, rivaling some of our favorite fictional shows like Grey-Sloan Memorial from Grey's Anatomy or Princeton-Plainsboro from House.

For a more budget-friendly stay in Kumasi, consider accommodations at the Kwame Nkrumah University of Science & Technology (KNUST), where you can book a room for as little as 360 cedis—less than $40 USD per night, including breakfast. And yes, these rooms are open to everyone, not just those affiliated with the university. In the Central Region, the University of Cape Coast offers unparalleled tropical scenery. With beaches just a stone's throw away, it's no wonder students might feel undeniably tempted to skip class for the surf and sand!

Uniquely uplifting umbrellas, bursting with unmistakable colors, are a sight to behold at Ghanaian celebrations and ceremonies, especially funerals! In the city of Asamankese, I had the unforgettable experience of attending a royal funeral in Anum-Asamankese, located in the Eastern Region. These umbrellas are uniquely designed to represent different cities, and the Chiefs dance proudly beneath them, as unwavering men rhythmically thrust them into the air. Funerals here are unlike any other—days-long celebrations of life that start as early as 5 a.m., with drumming, dancing, and DJs keeping the energy high late into the night! The entire community unites to honor and celebrate multiple members of the community who have recently passed away. Thank you to the chiefs of Anum-Asamankese for permission to capture this unforgettable event as "credentialed media."

One touching tradition is the presence of a table right on-site, where families can pay "community dues" to fund funeral expenses for any family in need. Even if you don't attend a funeral during your visit, you're sure to see these unmissable umbrellas at other vibrant celebrations, flapping magnificently in the breeze.

Utazi Leaf

Popular Food:

Utazi soup—made with with leaves of the Gongronema latifolium plant

Destination: **University of Ghana (Greater Accra region), University of Cape Coast (central region)**

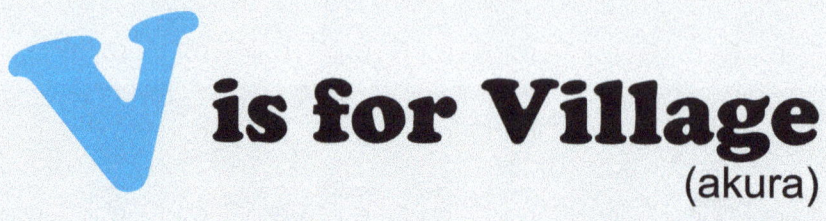 V is for Village
(akura)

Villages with traditional huts may be what you think of when you hear "Africa," but Villagio, an area boasting vertical views with tall apartments and even a rooftop restaurant offering vibrant vistas, is becoming more and more the vision as you venture across the growing metropolis of Accra.

My Starbucks crew may be visibly vexed, struggling for that morning coffee and breakfast pastry to get you going. However, you will be able to get your morning fix at any of 300 various Vida E Caffé locations throughout the African continent. I mean, the name is Portuguese for "life and coffee"—I truly believe they will have what you need to get you through while visiting. They offer vegan, vegetarian, halal, dairy-free, gluten-free, and wellness supplements. Another viable vegan venture for my plant-based lifestylers is the purely vegan Mahorgany Cafe, located at the A & C Mall in the heart of Accra. Mahorgany offers entrees such as mushroom and tofu fried rice and coconut curry spaghetti. They also have vibrant vegetable smoothies and salads that will make your taste buds sing.

V is for Visa—no, not the plastic card in your wallet to pay for things. I'm talking about a travel visa, which is required for entry into the country. The cost for a one-year single-entry or five-year multiple-entry visa is the same price: $100. Whether you intend to come just once or voyage multiple times, make sure you apply early and have at least three full weeks before travel—even if paying the extra $100 for expedited processing.

Since my travels, the nation has valiantly ventured into efforts to invite diasporans from America to come home by extending the option of visas on arrival for special time periods. Always be sure to check before you travel because these programs are often only temporary!

Vegetable Soup

Popular Food:

Vegetable soup—made with any variety of vegetables

Destination: Volta River (Volta region)

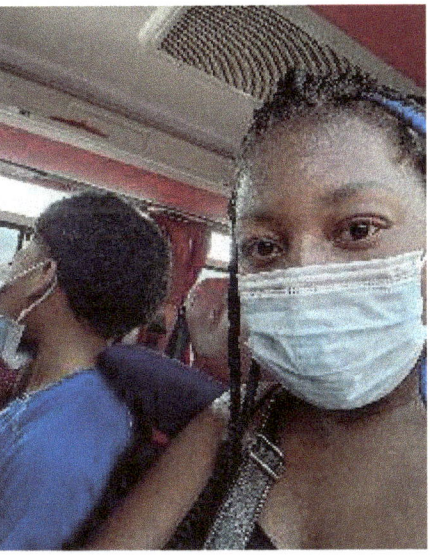

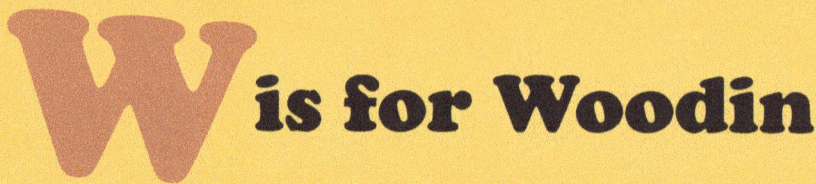 W is for Woodin

Wo ho te sɛn? "How are you?" "Me ho yɛ," meaning "I'm fine," and ready to explore Ghana! Engage with the warmth of the Ghanaian people by starting conversations with this friendly greeting. From bustling markets to serene villages, the phrase is your key to unlocking smiles and connections. Try it out as you go shopping for Woodin. Woodin is a brand celebrated for its vibrant, African-inspired fabrics that weave art and culture into every thread. With its signature shimmery finish, Woodin is a premium choice in Ghana, much like a Coach bag in the U.S. It's not the peak of luxury, but it's a polished step above the everyday, blending sophistication with cultural heritage. Wandering through a Woodin store is a wondrous experience, where patterns and prints speak stories of African identity and pride. Whether crafting custom attire or selecting a ready-made piece, Woodin wraps you in Ghanaian elegance.

Widen your worldview and immerse yourself in the wealth of wisdom at the W.E.B. Du Bois Center in Accra, established in 1985 to honor the life and legacy of the renowned scholar and civil rights leader. The center is home to the African American Association of Ghana (AAAG), now led by Queen Mother Nana Akosua Serwaa Seɛyɔ I, and features a museum, research library, and archives brimming with materials on African unity, Ghana's history, and the contributions of the African diaspora.

For nature lovers, witness the wonder of Ghana's waterfalls. Wli Falls, the tallest in West Africa, wows visitors with a rewarding hike through lush greenery to its cascading waters. Asenema Falls, closer to Accra, offers a welcoming escape for a serene retreat or adventurous outing.

Waakye

Popular Food:

Waakye (wah/chay/)— a wonderful wedding of rice and beans cooked together

Destination: **Waterfalls - (Wli Falls, Volta region); Asenema (Greater Accra region)**

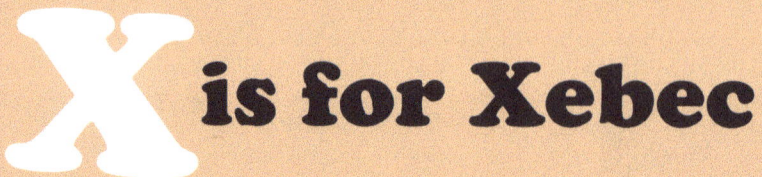X is for Xebec

A xebec—(zeh/buhk)-a type of sleek sailing ship—was once used in trade along the West African coast. These x-traordinary vessels were commonly employed by Europeans to exchange "exotic exports", (textiles, spices, and tragically enslaved people) between Ghana and other countries. The word "xebec" might make you scratch your head at first—what is THAT?? But once you see a picture, you'll likely have a lightbulb moment: "Oh, a slave ship!" The xebec's unique design allowed for efficient exploration and exchange, making it a cornerstone of coastal commerce during its time. While their history is marred by the exploitation of the transatlantic slave trade, xebecs symbolize both the triumph and turmoil of Ghana's historical relationship with the sea.

When you think of African music, the rhythmic resonance of the hand drum may come to mind. But let's not forget the exquisite, expressive xylophone, another percussion instrument with roots deeply embedded in the Motherland. Found primarily in the northern part of Ghana, the xylophone's extraordinary craftsmanship uses wooden keys that are struck with mallets to create euphonious, exotic tones.

Traditional Ghanaian folk music often features the xylophone's unique, exuberant sound, making it a staple of cultural performances. If you're eager to experience its captivating melodies, head to Accra's Abajo Café in the Arts Center, where you can enjoy local folk music performed live. Despite the dark legacy of slavery, iterations of the xylophone can also be found as far as South America, symbolizing how this timeless instrument has expanded its influence across the globe.

Xeri Porridge

Popular Food:

Xeri—a creamy cornmeal porridge with a smooth texture and a satisfying flavor

Destination: **X-traordinary Axim Beach Resort and Spa (Western region)**

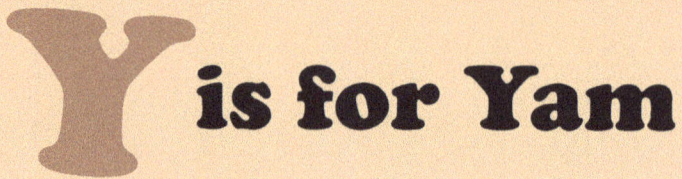Y is for Yam

Each Thanksgiving season, Black families across the United States engage in a yearly yam-versus-sweet-potato debate whose origins remain as mysterious as Grandma's secret pie recipe. However, after my trips to Ghana, I can safely put this debate to rest. In the U.S., that orange pie filler or marshmallow-topped casserole is NOT the African yam. The African yam is a yard-long, yellow-ish tuber with a rough, brown exterior that can be transformed into traditional dishes like yam porridge, fried yam balls, pounded yam for fufu, or even boiled and sliced to sop up okra or vegetable soups. You'll spot these yummy yams in markets or on street corners—giant, gnarled logs being toted to and fro by vendors.

Yango is another yes-worthy ride-share service in Greater Accra. You won't miss these cars' yawning red signs on their roofs to identify them. Simply download the app and you're ready to go!

And we cannot forget Nana Yaa Asantewaa, the yearning, yet unyielding Queen Mother of the Asante (Ashanti) people, who fearlessly led an army to defend the Golden Stool, the sacred throne of her people, against British forces on March 28, 1900. Her legacy looms large, and Viola Davis' portrayal in The Woman King is said to have been inspired by her courageous spirit.

Yellow Fever vaccination is another you-can't-skip step for travel prep. Vaccination against this disease is mandatory for entry into Ghana. It's probably your priciest pre-travel purchase, but here's the good news: once you're vaccinated, you're cleared to travel to many African countries for life.

Yam Chips

Popular Food:
Yam chips—sliced yam deep fried like French fries

Destination: **Yendi (Northern region)**

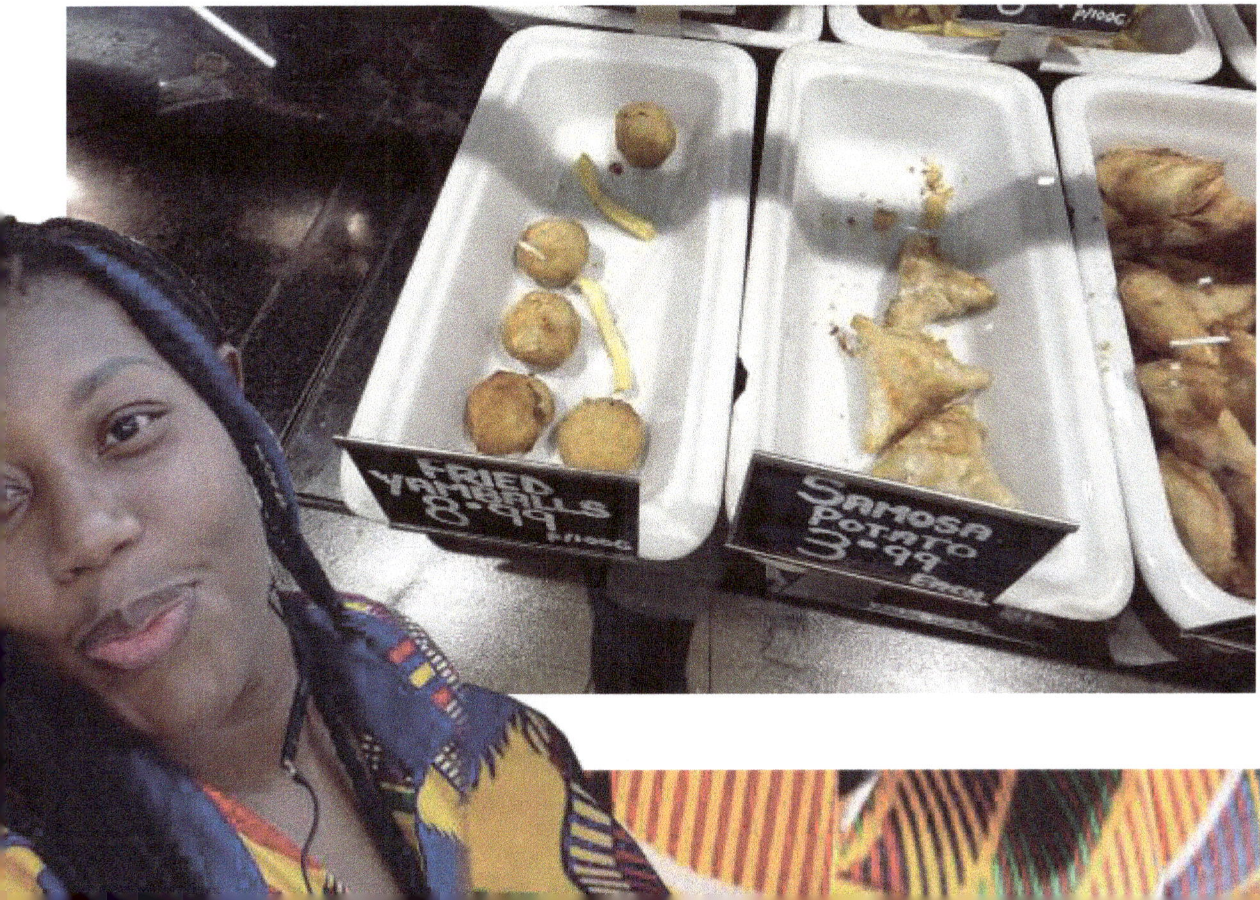

Z is for Zongo

Zongo is a term used to describe predominantly Muslim neighborhoods in Ghana's major cities. Zongo chiefs act as traditional leaders, presiding over the affairs of these communities. During my trip, it was fascinating to witness a small council meet-up one evening at Abajo Café, located on the premises of the Arts Center in Accra. Whether practicing the Muslim faith or not, you can't help but marvel at the many beautiful mosques across the country, their spires and domes rising high above the bustling city streets.

Contrary to popular belief, wildlife is not just roaming up and down the streets—unless, of course, we're talking about mosquitoes buzzing by (best not forget your DEET bug spray)! In Ghana (and Africa as a whole) just like in the United States, you will have to visit a zoo (mmoa yɛmmea) if you want to see wild animals.

We stopped by the Accra Zoo to check them out. Among the highlights were monkeys, snakes, crocodiles, lions, and the ever-majestic striped horses of the wild, known as zebras. You can also explore other zoos in Ada, accessible by a boat ride from the Aqua Safari Resort, or in Kumasi.

ZoomLion is a waste management company in Ghana that provides a range of services including waste collection, disposal, and recycling. Of the many comparisons that can be made to life in the U.S., this is a small but notable one you may spot as you drive through residential neighborhoods—modern solutions for an age-old issue.

Zomi

Popular Food:

Zomi—a vibrant red palm oil, specially cured and essential to many Ghanaian dishes.

Destination: **Zebilla (Upper East region) and Zabzugu (Northern region)**

A Globetrotter's Ghana Travel Index

Aburi Mountains   Region: Eastern

Accra Zoo   Region: Greater Accra

African American Association of Ghana (AAAG)   Region: Greater Accra

Aqua Safari Resort   Region: Greater Accra

Anum Asamankese   Region: Eastern

Asenema Waterfall   Region: Greater Accra

Assin Manso Slave River   Region: Central

Bliss Family Entertainment (bowling, trampoline park, and more)   Region: Greater Accra

Bloom Bar (night life)   Region: Greater Accra

Bonwire Kente Factory in Kumasi   Region: Ashanti

Botanical Gardens (Aburi)   Region: Eastern

Cape Coast Adventure Park (ziplining, canopy walk)   Region: Central

Cape Coast (beach, many resorts and castles)   Region: Central

Door of No Return   Region: Central

Estuary of Ada   Region: Greater Accra

Fort William   Region: Central

Freetown Chophouse (Sierra Leone cuisine) Region: Greater Accra

Ghana's other forts   Region: multiple cities and regions

Ho (sogli Yam Festival in September)   Region: Volta

Independence Square   Region: Greater Accra

Jirapa   Region: Upper West

Kakum National Park   Region: Central

Kwame Nkrumah Memorial Center   Region: Greater Accra

Labadi Beach   Region: Greater Accra

Larabanga Mosque   Region: Savannah

Linda Dor Highway Rest Stop   Region: Eastern

Makola Market   Region: Greater Accra

Manhyia Palace   Region: Ashanti

Mole National Park (safari)   Region: Northern

Navrongo   Region: Upper East (Burkina Faso border)

Osu district - (great for nightlife and shopping)   Region: Greater Accra

Peduase Valley Resort   Region: Greater Accra

Prampram Beach   Region: Greater Accra

Queen's Palace in Kumasi   Region: Ashanti

Rawlings Park Region: Greater Accra

Skybar (dinner/ night life) Region: Greater Accra

Sunyami   Region: Brong Ahafo (Burkina Faso border)

Tamale   Region: Northern

University of Cape Coast (Guest Housing offers reasonably priced lodging)   Region: Central

University of Ghana (Guest Housing offers reasonably priced lodging)   Region: Greater Accra

Vida e Caffe   Region: (multiple locations)

W.E.B. Du Bois Center at the African American Association of Ghana
Region: Greater Accra

Wli Falls   Region: Volta

Axim Beach Resort & Spa   Region: Western

Yendi - (explore Dagbon heritage and local markets)   Region: Northern

Zabzugu - (a quiet escape with local crafts and cultural treasures).   Region: Northern

Zebilla - (a charming town with scenic views)   Region: Upper East

American Support Organizations

American Institute for Resource & Human Development
Phone: 770-330-2780
Email: ameriresource1@gmail.com
https://american-resource.org/

African American Association of Ghana (located in Accra, Ghana)
https://aaaghana.org/
Email: aaagsecretary@gmail.com

American Vendors for African Goods & Services

Levonne Gigger Ekechukwu: SophistiTwerk Fitness LLC
Offering: shea butter & black soap
Phone # +1 (678) 870-7395
WhatsApp Phone # +1 (785) 317 2422
Email: stwerkclass@gmail.com
www.Sophistitwerk.com

NativWearhouse LLC
Offering: Graphics Design & Apparel Print Services
What'sApp Phone # +1 (770) 896-5654
Email: nativwearhouse@gmail.com

Wanda Gigger: Sites 2 C
Offering: Website creation & webmaster services, K-12 tutoring,
and voice-over acting
https://www.facebook.com/share/1FKHnehAHZ/?mibextid=wwXlfr

Linda Murphy Maina: Linda's Afrikan Kreations
Offering: African jewelry
Phone # +1 (785) 260-9172
What'sApp Phone # +1 (785) 640 4542
Email: lindasafrikankreations@gmail.com
https://www.facebook.com/LindasAfrikanKreations
https://www.instagram.com/LindasAfrikanKreations

Ghanaian Vendors
Education Services

Nanahemaa Dokua aka Christiana Odamea
Offering: Twi Tutoring
What'sApp Phone # +233 20 755 3845
 [instagram, facebook, website-optional]

Photographers

Alpha-Images
Offering: Photography and Videography related services
WhatsApp Phone #: +0 558 85 2067
Call: +0 50 082 4799
Email: fafashotit@gmail.com
Website:https://www.instagram.com/d_alphaimages/profilecard/?igsh=MWRuZTI1cGNzaG82
0A==

Seamstress Services

Jane Mensah: Mejane Fashion Designer
What'sApp Phone # +233 24 314 4807
https://www.instagram.com/mejane_fashion_desginer

Mavis OFM & Beatrice:
What'sApp Phone # +233 54 949 1230
https://www.instagram.com/mavisoforikwartemaa9207/

Travel & Tours

Jah King: JKROYALS TOURS VENTURES
Also Offering: drum and dance lessons, customized drum;
What'sApp Phone # +233 20 280 4592

Snapshots of Ghana: Creative Credits
Photo Credits & Attributions

We would like to extend our gratitude to the following for their contributions of personal photographs and permissions to take photos: The Chiefs of Anum Asamankese, Nana Dokua Odamea aka Christiana Odamea, Nana Jah King, and Onche Ugbabe.

We also thank the photographers whose creative commons images were used in this book.

Ampesi Image of Plantain Dish by Daniel Wiafe, used under Creative Commons Attribution-ShareAlike 4.0 License. Available at: https://upload.wikimedia.org/wikipedia/commons/c/c9/Plantain_dish.jpg.

Domedo Image of goat stew by Cookipedia, used under Creative Commons Attribution 4.0 International License. https://www.cookipedia.co.uk/wiki/images/thumb/d/d2/Goat_stew_slow_cooker_recipe_recipe.jpg/450px-Goat_stew_slow_cooker_recipe_recipe.jpg.

Gold: Image of Ashanti gold ornaments (mask and shield) by Public Domain, used under Creative Commons Public Domain Dedication (CC0 1.0 Universal). https://upload.wikimedia.org/wikipedia/commons/6/69/Gold_ornaments_%28mask_and_shield%29%2C_Ashanti_-African_objects_in_the_American_Museum_of_Natural_History-_DSC05964.JPG.

Ghana dancer: Image of dancing in Ghana by Ewais, used under Creative Commons Attribution-ShareAlike 4.0 International License. https://commons.m.wikimedia.org/wiki/File:Dancing_in_Ghana_4.jpg.

Ghana Flag Image of the Flag of Ghana by Wikimedia Commons user 'Stuntboy', used under Creative Commons Attribution-Share Alike 4.0 International License. https://commons.wikimedia.org/wiki/File:Flag_of_Ghana.png#file.

Haako millet porridge: Image of millet porridge by Wikimedia Commons user 'Ezoe,' used under Creative Commons Attribution 4.0 International License. https://commons.m.wikimedia.org/wiki/File:Millet_porridge.png.

Moi Moi - Image of moi moi with fresh fish and boiled egg by Bukky658, used under Creative Commons Attribution-Share Alike 4.0 International License. You can view the license at https://creativecommons.org/licenses/by-sa/4.0, via Wikimedia Commons.

Nungua Homowo Festival: Image of the Nungua Homowo Festival by Richest Kid, used under Creative Commons Attribution-Share Alike 4.0 International License. You can view the license at https://creativecommons.org/licenses/by-sa/4.0, via Wikimedia Commons

Omu tuo Image of omo tuo (rice balls) by Thomson200, used under Creative Commons CC0 License. You can view the license at https://creativecommons.org/licenses/by-sa/4.0, via Wikimedia Commons.

Quail Eggs Image of quail eggs in frying pan by Engin Akyurt, used under Pexels License. Available at: https://images.pexels.com/photos/6294316/pexels-photo-6294316.jpeg?auto=compress&cs=tinysrgb&w=1260&h=750&dpr=1

Queenmother Nana Dokua: Photo of Nana Dokua, used with permission.

Red Red: Image of 'Red Red' wrapped in Katemfe leaves (Thaumatococcus danielii) by Mwintirew, used under Creative Commons Attribution-ShareAlike 4.0 International License. Available at: https://upload.wikimedia.org/wikipedia/commons/8/8b/%22Red_Red%22_wrapped_in_Katemfe_leaves_%28Thaumatococcus_daniellii%29.jpg.

Tuo Zaafi: Image of Tuo Zaafi by Isaac Gyamfi Assumeng, used under Creative Commons Attribution-ShareAlike 4.0 International License. Available at: https://upload.wikimedia.org/wikipedia/commons/1/10/Tuo_Zaafi_2.png.

Utazi leaf: Image of Gnetum africanum leaves by Minette Lontsie, used under Creative Commons Attribution-ShareAlike 4.0 International License. Available at: https://upload.wikimedia.org/wikipedia/commons/d/d0/Gnetum_africanum_Leaves_%28Eru%2C_Okok%29.jpg.

Vegetable Soup: Image of Ademe soup by daSupremo, used under Creative Commons Attribution-ShareAlike 4.0 International License. Available at: https://upload.wikimedia.org/wikipedia/commons/9/9e/Ademe_soup.jpg.

xebec (ship): Image of Chebec Mistic by Rama, used under Creative Commons Attribution-ShareAlike 3.0 France License. Available at: https://upload.wikimedia.org/wikipedia/commons/a/ac/Chebec_Mistic-IMG_8860.jpg.

xeri: Image of Akamu (Pap/Ogi) by FOODIEAFRICAN, used under Creative Commons Attribution-ShareAlike 4.0 License. Available at: https://upload.wikimedia.org/wikipedia/commons/1/15/Akamu_%28Pap%29_%28Ogi%29_%28cropped%29.jpg.

Zomi (palm oil) Image of Palm Oil (Red Oil) by Flixtey, used under Creative Commons Attribution-ShareAlike 4.0 License. Available at: https://upload.wikimedia.org/wikipedia/commons/d/d8/Palm_Oil_%28Red_Oil%29.jpg.

www.ingramcontent.com/pod-product-compliance
Lightning Source LLC
Chambersburg PA
CBHW041520120626
46551CB00018B/2514